A gift for:

_____

From:

_____

SIMPLE SUGGESTIONS FOR

A
Sensational
Life!

Paula White

www.jcountryman.com
A division of Thomas Nelson, Inc.
www.thomasnelson.com

Paula

Published by the J. Countryman division of Thomas Nelson, Inc., Nashville, Tennessee 37214

Project manager—Terri Gibbs

ISBN: 1-4041-0293-0

Designed by The DesignWorks Group; cover, David Uttley; interior, Robin Black.
       www.thedesignworksgroup.com

www.thomasnelson.com
www.jcountryman.com
www.paulawhite.org

Printed in China

Contents

God intends for

His dream and destiny to be

fulfilled in you.

Leave the Past,
Walk into the Future

Is your past one that you wish you had never lived?

Is your past something that you want to continue to relive again and again?

You cannot enter your tomorrow as long as you hold on to your past.

Let go of your past.

Leaving the past behind does not mean that we only leave the negative aspects of the past behind. For some people, the struggle is in leaving behind a past that they perceive to be better than their present. There are some people who have trouble letting go of past success. Or they create a fantasized past and dwell in a set of false memories. The past—no matter what it is— needs to be left in the past!

You can't look backwards

and forward

at the same time.

Stop using what was
to determine what will be!

Your tomorrow does not have to be like your yesterday. Where you came from doesn't determine where you are going!

Too many people today are predicting their end based on their beginnings. In life the most important thing is not where you start, but where you finish. I am so thankful that God can interrupt a person's life and change the destiny of that person for His good. God does not use your past to determine your future . . . so why should you? It's a fallacy to plan your future only by comparing it to your past.

Don't miss out

on your opportunity to

experience God's best in your life

because you are focused on

the worst of your life.

Let God's love restore you!

When God restores you, He brings you to wholeness. He gives you the courage to love again . . . the courage to face life . . . the ability to experience life fully. Out of your wholeness, you are able to love the unlovable, be brave in the face of terror, and trust even after years of not being able to trust.

Open yourself up to God's restoring love.

Walk into your future.

God's Word tells us that we become new creatures the moment we accept Jesus as our Savior. That does not mean we instantly experience a new environment, new circumstances, new situations, or new relationships. There's a walking out and a working out that's our responsibility. We are the ones who have to create and establish a new atmosphere for our lives—an atmosphere that is focused on God and based on His Word.

We are the ones who

need to develop new circumstances

and new situations that are

good in God's eyes.

We are the ones who

need to form new relationships

that are godly, encouraging,

and beneficial.

If you continue to look back,

you won't be qualified

to possess what God has for you.

Look ahead, not back.

Don't look at what might have been,
should have been,
or could have been!
Look at what is still to be!

There may be a situation in which someone comes to you to break off a relationship. Allow that break to occur. Don't keep hanging on. Don't keep trying to mend fences that are twelve-foot-high stone walls. Don't keep revisiting the relationship in your heart, looking for a way back in. Allow the break to happen.

And then, move forward.

When God says "no" get up and say "yes" to the future He holds out to you.

You may have wept in anguish before God. Your heart may have been broken. You may have fasted and prayed. And in spite of anything you did or didn't do . . . God said no to that relationship, no to that miracle you wanted, no to that outcome you desired.

Who knows what good things God has for you in your future? Who knows the abundance of life He has for you? You won't know unless you rise up and walk toward your future!

Get up and pray.

Get up and read the Word.

Get up and take action!

You are a victor

not a victim.

Focus on the good things
God has done for you, is doing for you,
and will do for you.

Change your focus. You must change your focus as you leave your past and embrace your future. You must begin to see yourself in new ways.

Focus on your future. What you focus on is what captures your attention and your affection.

Our thoughts become our words.

Our words become our actions.

Our actions become our habits.

Our habits become our character.

Our character becomes our destiny.

Do not look behind.
Look ahead to where God
is leading you!

When thoughts about the brokenness of the
past come, we must resist them and press
toward wholeness.

When thoughts about past losses come—thoughts
about material things we may have lost or relationships
we may have lost—we must resist those thoughts and
press toward the future blessings God has for us.

A person who is pressing forward has to resist all
forms of fear, including the fear of the unknown.

Prioritize God

God does not save you
because He feels sorry for you.

He does not deliver you
because you are in a bad place.

He does not bless you
because you have great need.

God saves and delivers
and blesses because you cry out
to Him with your faith.

Believe that God is
Lord of heaven and earth.

Faith is an equal-opportunity business.

If you can believe . . .

God will rebuild your broken life.

If you can believe . . .

God will restore your broken home.

If you can believe . . .

God will remold your broken dreams.

Give God your faith.

God does not look at your past mistakes and exclude you from His promises. Neither does God give you His promises on the basis of any good works you have done. It is your faith in Him that brings God's promises to you.

God doesn't look at your résumé. He isn't impressed with your cuteness or your cleverness. God says, "If you will give me your faith, I will give you your future."

There is therefore now

no condemnation to those who are

in Christ Jesus, who do not

walk according to the flesh,

but according to the Spirit.

ROMANS 8:1

See God for who God is.

We can never fully know all the infinite facets of an eternal God, but we can know that God is more than anything we will ever become. We see God as being all-powerful, all-wise, all-loving, and eternal.

See Him as your rock among the shifting sands of life.

See Him as the balm of Gilead in the midst of your sickness.

See Him as your provider in the midst of your lack.

See Him as eternal and unchanging in the midst of your busy life.

The more you see who God is,

the more you see who He is to you.

The more you see who God is to you,

the more you see how

valuable you are to Him!

You can't praise God and worry at the same time.

You can't praise God and be anxious at the same time.

You can't praise God and be frustrated at the same time.

Devote your life
to praise.

Praise brings us face-to-face with the truth of God's love for us. The more you praise God for who He is, the more you are confronted by His infinite and unchanging care, provision, and protection. In praise you come to recognize more clearly God's righteousness, holiness, mercy, forgiveness, and grace.

In praise, you come to know His love.

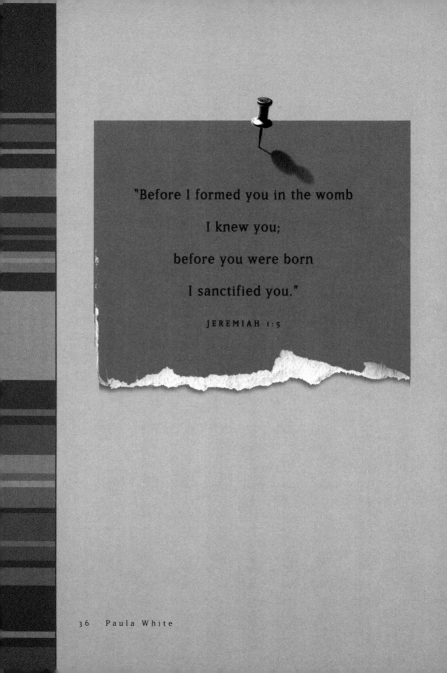

"Before I formed you in the womb

I knew you;

before you were born

I sanctified you."

JEREMIAH 1:5

Discover God's assignment
for your life.

You were not "created" by your mother and father. You were created by God, who formed and fashioned you long before you were in the womb of your mother.

God gave you the color of eyes you have. He gave you the color of skin you have. He gave you the DNA that you have—your genetic makeup. He gave you the intelligence that you have, the ability to commune that you have, the personality you have. God designed you perfectly for the assignment on your life.

The God who has prepared

the blessing for you

is the God who is preparing you

for the blessing.

Look yourself in the mirror and say:

I am not a product of my past.

I am not a product of my environment.

I am not who other people say that I am.

I am who God says I am.

I am who God is calling me to be.

Embrace what the Word of God has to say about you.

Bring your life into alignment with what the Word of God says about you—that's the pattern for your life.

Get into the Word.

Study the Word.

Memorize the Word.

Speak the Word.

Meditate on the Word.

Act on the Word.

God does not discriminate, but freely and generously pours out His gifts to all people.

Know that you are loved by God.

When you know that you are loved by God, you aren't nearly as concerned about who might not love you.

When you know that you are valued by God, you aren't nearly as concerned about who might not value you.

When you know that God calls you beloved and worthy, you aren't nearly as concerned about what other people might call you.

He who has begun

a good work in you

will complete it

until the day of Jesus Christ.

PHILIPPIANS 1:6.

Never forget that God has called you for an eternal purpose.

Where you are right now, is not where you will be. You will continue to increase as you go from glory to glory. Do not miss God's assignment for your life. He has a plan for you.

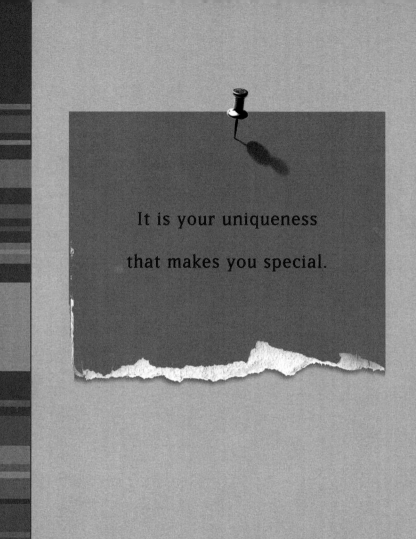

It is your uniqueness

that makes you special.

Acknowledge the gifts
God has given you.

God chose all the attributes for your life, and He knew where to put you, with whom to put you, and how to place you in time and space so that He might raise you up to be a witness of His love and power to this world.

People who don't know that they are God's workmanship often spend a very long time trying to be something they were not created to be. They try to change their appearance and their talents. They try to bypass their culture or their ethnicity or their gender. God made you, and He made you "fearfully and wonderfully" (Ps. 139:14).

Seek God's wisdom before you make any major decision.

We make bad decisions when we don't seek God's wisdom before making major decisions and choices. Seek out godly mentors and counselors for advice.

Without God's direction

we open ourselves a revolving door

of trial and failure.

So do it right the first time

by seeking God's wisdom.

God is

as big as

you allow Him

to be.

Take the limitations off God!

If you believe God to heal a cold, He'll heal a cold.

If you believe God to heal cancer, He'll heal cancer.

If you believe God to raise the dead, He'll raise the dead.

If you believe God to save your family, He'll save your family.

If you believe God to save your community, He'll save your community.

If you believe God to shake nations, He'll shake nations.

How big is your God?

Faith is what empowers you

to obtain all that

God has promised you.

Ask God for big things.
Believe God for big things.

S top waiting for someone to come along and help you out. Pursue what God has for you. Trust God! Get going! Expect something significant to happen! He has so much in store for you.

Persevere in prayer.
God will answer you.

That answer may come as you read God's Word . . . as you hear a sermon on television, in church, or at a conference . . . or it may come from the still, small voice of God speaking in your heart. The answer may come into your mind and heart in a flash, or it may come to you slowly over time. But the answer will come.

God hears and God answers. When you call upon Him, He will answer you.

What God says will be,

will be.

Trust God,
no matter what!

Faith causes you to call things that are not as though they were and to call things that are as though they were not.

So let the weak say, "I am strong."

Let the poor say, "I am rich."

Let the barren say, "I am fruitful."

Let the sick say, "I am healed."

I trust You.

I trust You.

I trust You!

Step into the blessings God has for you.

Instead of infirmity . . . our heavenly Father gives us wholeness.

Instead of wandering . . . our heavenly Father gives us direction and destiny, purpose and fulfillment.

Instead of mourning and sadness over what has been . . . our heavenly Father gives us joy about what can be and what will be.

Instead of low self-worth . . . our heavenly Father tells us we are valuable.

Instead of a devalued, hopeless,

and helpless feeling that we are nothing and

never will be anything . . .

our heavenly Father gives us love

and counts us so valuable

that He sent His only Son to die on a cross

so we could live with Him forever.

Build Good
Relationships

Accept only what God says about you,

and the words of those

who align themselves with

His proclamations over your life!

Don't let others define you.

If you allow other people to define you, they'll limit you—they'll define you in a way that is less than what God has for you. They'll define you as less successful than God wants you to be. They'll define you as less blessed, less intelligent, less effective, and less spiritual than God wants you to be. If you allow them to define you and limit you, you truly will be limited! You won't press forward into the fullness of what God says you can be.

Know who you are in Christ.

Don't demand from people what only God can give.

O nly God can give you a deep awareness of how infinitely valuable and precious you are to Him, and what a glorious destiny He has for you.

Only God can see and meet the unfulfilled needs in your life that even you don't recognize.

Only God can fix your heart.

Only God can mend your mind.

There are cares that only God
can take on His shoulders!

There are bondages only
God can break.

There are situations only God
can resolve.

There are circumstances only
God can change.

God's ultimate plan

for you

is always good.

Never compromise
your character for anyone.

There are relationships that prey on your heart and rob you of control over your life. Don't give power to any person to manipulate and control you. Nobody deserves that power but God! No person can make you lose your joy, your mind, your temper, or any other aspect unless you give that person the power. Don't do it!

Never lose your identity for

another person's sake.

A healthy relationship is one in which

there is balance. There is give and take and

there is mutual appreciation

and a building up of each other.

It is one in which honest

words of appreciation are exchanged

without any hint of manipulation.

Cut unhealthy relationships
out of your life.

Trust God to help you recognize when a relationship is becoming detrimental to your business, your ministry, or the health of your family life. Trust God to give you the courage to end the relationship, and then trust Him to give you broad enough shoulders and thick enough skin to take the criticism that you may face for ending the relationship.

It takes emotional energy to end a relationship, and if you cut every unhealthy relationship out of your life at one time, you are likely to be overwhelmed by the loss. Cut unhealthy relationships out of your life one at a time until you can look around you and say, "All of my relationships are pleasing to God."

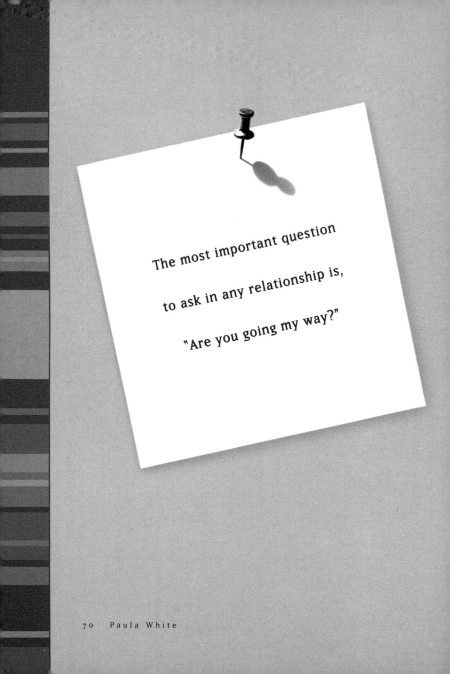

The most important question
to ask in any relationship is,
"Are you going my way?"

Form relationships based upon a common direction.

Y ou must be in relationship with people who have a common direction—common values and goals. If you do not have a common direction, you will always be in conflict.

To have the same destination

is to have a

conscious commitment

to a common goal.

Form relationships based upon the same destination.

God tells us very clearly that He has a deliberate destination for us as His children. Jeremiah 29:11 declares: "I know the thoughts that I think toward you," says the LORD, "thoughts of peace, and not of evil, to give you a future and a hope." God's thoughts toward us are for peace, which in Hebrew is Shalom. It literally means thoughts of safety, wellness, happiness, great health, prosperity, favor, rest, and completeness. In other words, "nothing missing and nothing broken" in your life.

Are the people you choose to have in your life going toward your same destination?

Recognize that no other human being can ever complete you.

Only God can do that work. Make the choice to accept and experience His love. Praise Him for His love. Grow in His love. And then begin to share His love.

Find your place in the love of God,

and you'll find your place

in the hearts of

those God puts in your life.

Don't try to be all things to all people.

God wants to work through you to help others, but He never wants you to try to take on the role of the Holy Spirit, or to be the end-all and be-all for another person.

Are you trying to change or fix someone?

Ask yourself, "Do I need to be needed by that person? Is the need I'm trying to fill a need that the Lord desires to fill? Am I standing in the way of God doing His work in him or her?"

Give your children over to the Lord . . .

and let God be God in their lives.

Give your marriage over to the Lord . . .

and let God be God in your spouse's life.

Worship the Father in spirit and truth; for the Father is seeking such to worship Him.

JOHN 4:23

Don't let anyone
keep you from God.

Have you ever been misunderstood in your worship? Have you ever been persecuted for your walk with God?

Have you ever been called names for taking a stand for Christ Jesus?

Have people ever made fun of you for going to church or giving your tithes and offerings or clapping your hands and dancing as you praise God?

Don't waste your strength fighting your critics—continue to bless the Lord!

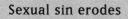

Sexual sin erodes

a person's self-worth.

Avoid every sexual encounter that is not blessed by God's commandments.

We treat vessels—bowls, vases, pitchers, and so forth—based upon our discernment of their value. We freely handle a plastic pitcher that costs two or three dollars, but we handle with extreme care the ornate porcelain vase that costs two or three thousand dollars. The same is true for the way we handle our physical bodies, which are also vessels.

Those who freely give themselves sexually to others do so because they do not value their bodies. When you do not value your body, you do not value your entire self.

Get to know your intended spouse extremely well before entering into the covenant of marriage.

Many people falsely market themselves—especially while dating. They sell themselves as beautiful, quiet, meek, and laid back. Then two years into the marriage they have an "in your face" attitude. You need to know a person before you enter into covenant with them. How does he treat people he doesn't need in his life? What does she value?

So many people end up falling for the exterior packaging and don't pay enough attention to the gift inside. They spend years, decades, even their lifetimes trying to change the person they married on the inside— but you cannot change a person, that's God's job.

The genuine person is not

the outside package,

but the treasure, gifting, and value

that lie within.

Associate with people who will encourage you.

God's Word says, "A friend loves at all times" (Proverbs 17:17).

A true friend will not despise your weakness, but will believe for your strength.

A true friend will not look down on you because of your past sin or failure, but will believe for your future glory in Christ Jesus.

A true friend will encourage you.

Put some distance

between yourself and those

who speak discouragement

into your life.

Pride goes

before destruction,

and a haughty spirit

before a fall.

PROVERBS 16:18

Be willing to say, "I'm sorry."

Why is it so hard for a person to say, "I'm sorry"? Pride.

We make all sorts of excuses: "He never says he's sorry, so why should I say I'm sorry?" "I was right, so why should I say I'm sorry?" "Sorry doesn't mean anything, so why say it?" That's wrong thinking. It doesn't matter what the other person says or doesn't say. Say "I'm sorry" a thousand times if you need to. Take the high road and pursue peace. "Seek peace and pursue it." (1 Pet.3:11)

If a person is

standing in the rain,

give him an umbrella.

Meet a need,
when you can.

Associate yourself with people who are troubled by the troubles of others and who move to help them. The day will come when you need a friend who will show mercy and compassion toward you. Strive to be a person of mercy and compassion.

Meeting the needs of others will put you in a position to receive what God has for you.

Find a person who is
worth following and make a place
for that person in your life.

None of us makes it alone or on our own. We follow
those who have gone before. We follow those who
are more mature. We follow teachers and mentors and
leaders. We follow preachers and pastors. We follow
those who lead.

Not every leader can take you where God wants you
to go. A leader cannot believe for something in your life
that he doesn't believe for his own life. He can't take you
to a place he doesn't believe you can go.

Are you following a leader who helps you to see more
than you can see? Are you following someone who can
help you experience God in a way that's beyond what
you've ever experienced?

Trust God to send

the right leader to lead you

into your destiny.

When it comes to

serving other people,

every person is

worthy of your best.

Serve with joy the leaders God has assigned to you.

When you know that you have been assigned by God to serve and learn from someone, you are willing to put up with all kinds of difficulties that come to distract you from that relationship. You are willing to do all kinds of jobs and put up with all kinds of hardships because you know without a doubt that God has called you to that relationship to teach you, prepare you, and ultimately, to bless you for your obedience.

God is preparing you for something greater than you can imagine!

Make a decision to walk
in agreement with the significant
people in your life.

To come into unity means to come into agreement. Agreement means "to pursue a conscious decision to work together and meet by appointment."

Regularly affirm your "agreement" to the significant people God has placed in your life.

We are not always "gentle and loving" to the people we consider different from us.

But without unity and agreement, there is no blessing.

"Be at peace among yourselves."
1 Thessalonians 5:13

Everybody that

passes your way

isn't worth

a second look.

Associate with people who are adding and multiplying your life.

There are four types of people in your life:

people who add

people who subtract

people who multiply

people who divide

Associate only with people who add or multiply your life. If a person is subtracting or dividing, you need to separate from that person

Don't try to be God to another person.

There's a huge difference between helping a person and carrying a person. You aren't the Holy Spirit. Don't enter into an enabling relationship in which you come to feel totally responsible for a person's success or failure.

God wants you to help others, but never take on the sole responsibility for their lives. God wants to have that position of responsibility so He can have that position of authority.

Ultimately . . .

Only God is able to be there always

for another person.

Only God is able to meet all needs.

Only God is able to

heal, restore, deliver, and bring a

person to wholeness.

Embrace your distinctiveness!

That's where

you'll find your value.

See your life from God's point of view.

Many people don't value themselves because they are looking to other people to set the standards for their lives. They are living by comparison—looking to people around them or to models in magazines to tell them what they should be, and by comparison, pointing out to them what they aren't. The truth is, you are the Designer's original.

You are not a cheap imitation of someone else. You are not a copy. You have your own specific physical identity—your own fingerprints and voiceprint and footprints and genetic code.

Manage Your Life

Like an airplane, you can only carry

so much weight. If you have too much baggage

on board, you will be unable to soar.

Manage your life
according to God's principles.

We must manage our time, which means our schedules. We need to take a look at each day and say, "There are only so many hours. How can I use them best to pursue the priorities I have set?"

We must manage our energy. Some tasks and relationships take more energy—physical, emotional, and spiritual—than others.

We must manage our creativity. We must focus it for the greatest impact and effectiveness.

Choose to follow God's instructions.

God's commands are laid out before us as a choice—we can choose whether we will obey or disobey.

They are laid out to us for our blessing, so that we might live and multiply and possess all God has for us.

They are laid out with consequences. If we choose not to obey the instructions God gives us, we face the consequences of our rebellion.

"My thoughts

are not your thoughts,

nor are your ways

My ways."

ISAIAH 55:8

We love people to

the degree that

we love ourselves.

Love yourself as much as you love others.

Besides your relationship with Jesus, the most important relationship you can have is your relationship with yourself. What you believe about yourself and the way you treat yourself will determine what you believe about others and the way you treat them!

You must begin to celebrate yourself. Only you know how far you have come to be the "you" that you are today!

Audit your priorities.

There are only so many pieces in a pie. There's only so much energy you can expend. There's only so much time you can allot. And there's only so much of yourself that you can give. And sooner or later, something or somebody is going to get the "crumbs" instead of a whole piece of pie. In nearly all cases, that "somebody" is the person who is slicing up the pie and handing out the pieces!

Set realistic expectations

for yourself.

Know what you can do.

Know how much you can do.

You can't conquer

what you will not confront.

And you can't confront

what you don't identify.

Identify and confront anything that keeps you from being successful in God's eyes.

E ach of us bears the responsibility of looking in the mirror and dealing with what we see there.

If you are willing to identify, confront, and conquer the issues of your life—to truly deal with them—God will heal you, restore you, and lead you into the destiny that He has planned for you, a destiny that is beyond your wildest dreams.

Is your "yes" always a yes, and your "no" always a no?

Do you live a life of integrity?

Do you accept God's authority over you and choose to follow His instructions?

Bind yourself to Christ Jesus
in a way that no person
and no circumstance
and no force can "undo" you.

Watch out for the slippery slope of ambivalence or disobedience. The enemy doesn't come with a temptation to deny Christ or to renounce God. The enemy comes with a temptation to move away from a close, intimate "knowing" of God just a little bit here, a little bit there, one decision, one commitment, and one choice at a time.

Start mastering
what is mastering you.

Have you ever been in a café and had a waitress pour you a cup of coffee as she said, "Tell me when"? If you don't tell her "when," she can pour until that cup overflows and coffee is all over the table. If you don't tell her "when," you can end up with a mess.

You have to learn how to say, "When."

People will keep dumping and dumping and dumping and dumping into your life unless you say, "No more!" Don't rely on others to notice when your cup is filled.

You must be the monitor

of your own

needs and limitations.

Audit your life.

Take a good look at the withdrawals and deposits of your time, energy, creativity, commitment, and resources. If there are more withdrawals than deposits, you are operating your life in the red, and sooner or later, something is going to break, fail, or fall apart. The damage may be to your health, to an endeavor you consider to be very important, or to relationships that you value highly. Making too many withdrawals and not enough deposits is going to leave you feeling "bankrupt"—empty, discouraged, and exhausted.

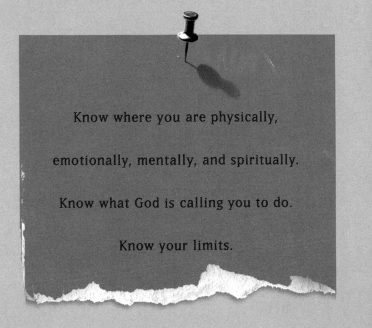

Know where you are physically,

emotionally, mentally, and spiritually.

Know what God is calling you to do.

Know your limits.

Who's the captain
of your vessel?

Learn to Say, "No."

You have a decision to make about every opportunity, challenge, or request that comes your way—say "yes" or say "no."

"No" is a complete sentence. If you want to be a little more polite in saying no, you might say, "No, thank you." But you must be firm in saying no when something that comes your way does not fall into your limited set of priorities and does not help you fulfill God's purpose for your life. You must be willing to say no regardless of who asks. You must say no when saying yes will cause a withdrawal of your time, energy, and commitment that cannot be balanced with an adequate deposit of time, energy, and commitment.

Live a balanced life.

Balance is a learning process. We each have to learn to live in balance.

The beginning of that learning comes with a recognition that we are triune beings—spirit, soul, and body.

The spirit has a need for both taking in nourishment and giving out ministry.

The mind has a need for both tranquillity and stimulation.

The body has a need for both rest and exercise.

Overloaded people fail.

Take time to replenish what
has been depleted in your life.

At times we need to rest. To rest physically means to sleep, to exert ourselves less, to attempt fewer physical chores. It might mean we need to go less and stay home more. To rest emotionally and mentally means to stop thinking about some things so much. It doesn't mean we stop caring, but it might mean we do stop caring so much. We turn our cares over to the Lord, asking the Lord to take care of the person in ways we cannot. To rest spiritually is to trust God to provide for us and others what we are wearing ourselves out trying to provide!

If you are depleted spiritually,

then you need to take time to

replenish yourself spiritually.

If you are depleted emotionally,

you need to do those

things that fill you up emotionally.

If you are depleted physically,

you need to do what's

necessary to restore your body.

God designed us to have

a day of praise and thanks

and quiet meditation on His Word.

He designed us to have a day

in which we gather with others to

praise and give thanks and

to study His Word.

Work six days
and rest one day.

God "rested" on the seventh day of creation, not because He was tired but because He was setting into motion by example His desire that man experience restoration, replenishment, and refreshment. God designed us to work six days and rest one day. He designed us to have a rhythm in our lives in which we have a time totally devoted to restoring what has been given out, replenishing what has been used up, receiving back what has been spent, and refreshing what has grown stale. He designed us so that our deepest form of restoration, replenishment, and refreshment is to come in relationship to Him.

Our lives move in the

direction of our

most dominant thoughts.

Let the mind of Christ
be in you.

God cares a great deal about how we think! He wants us to be whole in our minds. That's why His Word says, "Let this mind be in you which was also in Christ Jesus" (Phil. 2:5).

Let your thoughts reflect Christ.

Let His creative ideas become your creative ideas.

Let His attitudes become your attitudes.

Let His behavior become your behavior.

When you are wounded, give yourself permission to hurt and to express pain.

The expression of pain is part of the grieving process every person needs to go through after he or she has been hurt or suffered a loss. Grieving is vital to our coming to closure. Grieving is part of the healing process anytime we have lost something precious to us.

The loss may have been the loss of a loved one.

The loss may have been the loss of innocence.

The loss may have been a loss of self-worth, self-identity, or dignity.

A person who suffers any kind of loss needs to grieve.

Who can wipe a tear
that does not fall?

There's no sin beyond
the boundaries
of God's faithfulness
to forgive.

Take personal responsibility
for your own behavior.

Get honest with yourself and take responsibility for your life: "I did it. I was wrong. I messed up. I rebelled against You, God. I was in disobedience to You. Please forgive me."

There isn't any sin you've committed, mistake you've made, or weakness you've manifested that can't be forgiven. First John 1:9 tells us, "If we confess our sins, He is faithful and just to forgive us our sins and to cleanse us from all unrighteousness."

Know your position
in Christ Jesus.

The moment you begin to understand the mystery of God, and when His plan for your life begins to be unveiled before you, you will have a new energy flowing through you. You will have the power to straighten up on the inside and on the outside. You will have a new posture, a new bearing, a new dignity. When you begin to understand who loves you and who has adopted you into His family, you'll have a new identity, a new strength.

Knowing your position in Christ Jesus gives you the power to overcome any condition related to your past. When you know your position, your old "condition" has no power over you.

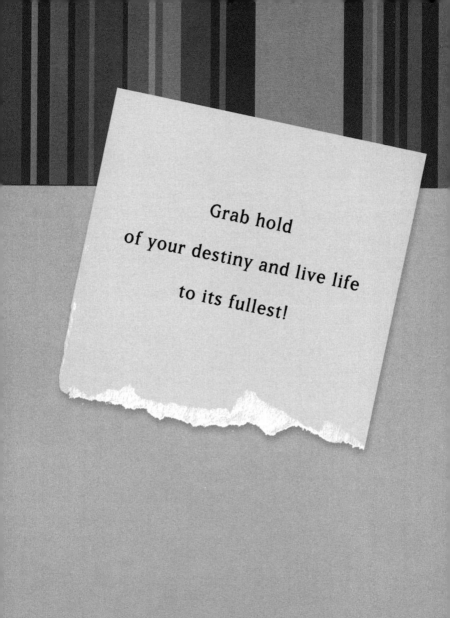

Grab hold
of your destiny and live life
to its fullest!

Keep your self-esteem
rooted in Christ.

God redeemed you for a reason. He redeemed you for a purpose. He redeemed you so you can fulfill His assignment for your life. God sees you as useful. He has a mission for you to accomplish!

He designed you from start to finish.

Even before anybody else accepted you,
He accepted you.

Even before anybody else loved you, He loved you.

Choose God's choice.

God gives you a chance to make a choice. But He tells you which choice to make!

It's up to you to choose His choice!

You have to shut the door to disobedience.

You have to open the door to obedience.

Choose what gives life.

Choose what is good.

Choose what produces blessing.

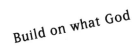

Build on what God

has built in you.

Embrace your God-given strengths.

Don't let anyone make you but God. Don't let the world put you in its cookie-cutter mold. If you give in to the way the world defines you, you will miss out on your unique qualities—the very qualities that make you valuable. What makes an antique or an artifact valuable? The fact that it is rare and distinct!

If God made you beautiful, use your beauty.

If God made you brainy, work your brain.

If God made you a computer genius, then work behind that computer to the glory of God.

If God made you a "natural" at business, then make a billion dollars to further of the kingdom of God!

The strength of what we do

flows out of what we think or believe

we are capable of doing.

We simply don't attempt things

we don't think we can do.

Make sure your dominant thoughts come from God's Word not man's opinion.

B ehavioral scientists tell us that a negative thought attached to a feeling can be repeated in a person's mind as many as six hundred times a day! It becomes what is called a dominant thought. And dominant thoughts drive behavior. They end up driving your entire life.

Are your dominant thoughts coming from God's Word or man's opinion?

When you know who you are, you develop a very solid self-esteem. You believe in yourself because you believe in what God says you are, what you are capable of doing, and what you can have.

Accept the dignity and value that God has placed on you.

H as a label been put on your life? Incapable? Inferior? Failure?

People are labelled all the time, even born-again Christians.

But the Word of God is higher than any natural or man-made law. It tells you who you are, what you can do, and what you can have.

If the Word of God says it . . . I can have it.

If the Word of God says it . . . I can be it.

If the Word of God says it . . . I can do it.

God's Word brings
to wholeness the person
to whom it is sent.

Replace life's lies with God's Word.

When you commit your ways to the Lord, He speaks all of His promises into your life.

That Word of the Lord breathed into your spirit causes something to happen. It causes something new to be birthed in you . . . and brought to the bud stage . . . and brought to the harvest stage of producing "seed" or "grain" . . . and brought to the fulfillment stage in which that grain is turned into "bread" that nourishes and satisfies your deepest desires. His Word once sent does not return void. It accomplishes what God sends it to do.

Step out on God's Word
and obey it.

You must initiate or act upon what God has promised to you. The Bible says, "Be doers of the word, and not hearers only, deceiving yourselves" (James 1:22).

Sow seeds.

Start giving.

Start helping others.

What you make happen for others,

God will make happen for you.

Trouble is an

incubator for greatness

Let the pressures you experience push you into God's power.

The Lord knew exactly the pressure you needed to get you to the place you are.

He knows the pressure it will take for you to birth what He has for you in your future.

He knows exactly what forces need to come against you and how to deliver you from them, so that by your coming up against those forces and experiencing God's delivering power, you are strengthened for what lies ahead. It is the pressure you have experienced that pushes you into God's power.

Don't be a complainer.

Complaining is a trap. Complainers never rise above or move beyond those things that are the focus of their complaint. God calls us to be "praisers." When you praise, you raise. This is especially true in times of adversity. When you praise, you raise your eyes from the problem to the Problem Solver. When you praise, you get your eyes off what is wrong and on the goal of what can be right. When you praise, you get your focus off the adversity and on the blessing that God has ahead for you.

If you complain,

you remain.

If you praise,

you raise.

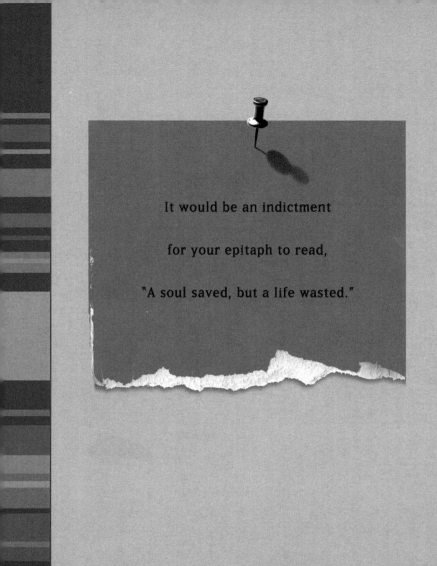

It would be an indictment

for your epitaph to read,

"A soul saved, but a life wasted."

Put your faith
into action.

P assive people don't win in life. People expect that after they become Christians, everything will fall out of heaven into their laps. But God's Word tells us that we become prosperous and successful when we speak God's Word, meditate on it day and night, and keep or observe it (Joshua 1:8). It takes effort to speak, effort to read and study and meditate on God's Word, and effort to do that every day, day in and day out.

Ultimately, what's going to matter is the quality of life we live, the character we develop, and the legacy we leave. What a shame to die without ever living!

Embrace
Your Dream

No one can

define your dream but you.

God gives your dream

to you alone.

Discover the destiny
God has created for you.

One of the greatest gifts you have in your life is the ability to see beyond your present state—to dream. As long as you are alive, there is a dream within you. You may not label it as such, but I assure you there is a dream within you—and it is all about God's great purposes and plans for your life and the lives you will touch as you fulfill the destiny He has designed for you.

Make sure your dream
is born of the Spirit.

Soulish dreams originate in your soul—your mind, will, or emotions. They are the dreams you dream for yourself, and they can have their source in some kind of fantasy.

On the other hand, God's dreams for you are birthed in the realm of the Spirit of God. They are planted in your heart by the Holy Spirit, and they are nourished by His ministry in your life.

We don't encounter God in fantasy;

we encounter God in real life.

Let go of the soulish fantasies

in your heart so there is

room for the dreams of God.

Devote your time and energy

to developing yourself

from the inside out.

Invest in what God has put inside you.

D on't invest in what fades. Invest in what lasts all through life and on into eternity! God doesn't want emotional nuclear waste inside you to spew out of you and contaminate others around you. He doesn't want hatred, anger, bitterness, or criticism flowing out of you. He doesn't want a controlling, manipulative spirit flowing from you. God wants the inside of you to be a "river of living water" flowing out to minister life and refreshment to others (see John 7:38).

Wisdom is the

comprehensive insight into the

ways and purposes of God.

Get God's wisdom for your life!

Knowledge comes from study, but wisdom comes from God. Every one of us needs more of God's wisdom. God's Word tells us, "If any of you lacks wisdom, let him ask of God, who gives to all liberally and without reproach, and it will be given to him" (James 1:5). We must do the asking. Only God can give us the insight and understanding about how to walk in His ways and accomplish His destiny for our life.

Pursue the dream
God has put in your life.

There's no difference between your "true" self and God's plan for you. Your true self is made up of your deepest desires and gifts and abilities and dreams and passions. Your true self is what God created in you. It is who God made you to be.

Selfishness is not a matter of pursuing your true self. Selfishness is when you stop giving to others and when you keep all of the harvest you reap for your own pleasures.

Instead of accepting the limits

that have been placed on you

(including the limits

you have placed on yourself)

challenge the system and

pursue your passion!

You are not a product

of what has happened to you

or what other people have said about you.

You are the sum total of

what is in you and Who is in you.

Value the gifts
God has given you.

God's Word says, "We have this treasure in earthen vessels, that the excellence of the power may be of God and not of us" (2 Cor. 4:7). What God has put in you is treasure. That word in the Greek means a deposit of wealth . . . of value. Treasure is what God has given you as your gifts and talents. It is the Spirit that God has placed in you.

Why do you have this treasure? That the "excellence of the power of God" might be manifested in your life.

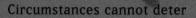

Circumstances cannot deter

what God promises . . .

and a change of circumstances cannot

bring about His promise.

Don't become impatient with God's timing!

Many times, God promises us things and rather than wait until He gives those things to us, we become anxious and attempt to make things happen. We try to manipulate people and situations, but in the end, all we create is a mess. God knows the precise timing for the fulfillment of the things He has promised us and prepared as our destiny. Nothing can stand in the way of His bringing to pass what He wills.

When you get discouraged, go to God's Word.

Anytime you think you might not make it, you need to remind yourself of God's Word:

- "In all these things we are more than conquerors through Him who loved us" (Rom. 8:37).
- "Now thanks be unto God, who always leads us in triumph in Christ, and through us diffuses the fragrance of His knowledge in every place" (2 Cor. 2:14).
- "For whatever is born of God overcomes the world. And this is the victory that has overcome the world—our faith" (1 John 5:4).

Our strength comes from God—

it's not something we work up in ourselves.

We can do all things through Christ.

It is God's strength poured into us and

working through us that enables us

to overcome, to persevere, and to be strong.

We come to strength by resting in Him.

The Word of God separates you

from the world and

consecrates you for service.

Use the power of God's Word to reach your destiny.

God's Word is the most powerful source in the world today. When things stand in your way and try to prevent you from reaching the destiny God has for you, His Word smashes those roadblocks away.

God's Word will keep your thoughts in check when your flesh wants to chase something that is not good for you; and it will protect you when your eyes see something that would put you in harm's way.

God's Word confronts and obliterates the devil's lies. It keeps you from being deceived.

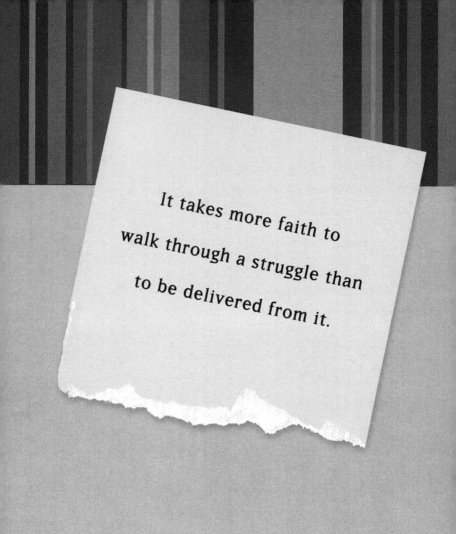

It takes more faith to walk through a struggle than to be delivered from it.

Never give up!

No matter what comes your way, you can make it become a pathway to destiny. Whatever you do, never give up.

The process of faith is the ability to endure. Your faith is dependent upon your ability to trust, and your level of trust is determined by your relationship with Christ.

Fill your life with faith by getting to know God!

The enemy wants to destroy

the dream inside of you.

Protect your dream.

The most effective way to safeguard your dream is to walk in the Spirit.

Stay clean before the Lord,

renew your mind by the Word,

apply godly wisdom,

PRAY,

worship,

and TRUST God.

Keep moving in
the direction of your dream.

No matter how difficult it may be, just get up and take a step forward.

Even when you don't feel like it, trust God enough—and believe in your dream enough—to do *something* to move toward it. Whatever you do, don't stop!

Always keep

moving toward what

God has for you.

By the power of your words,

your tongue becomes a pen

that writes your book of destiny.

Speak words of life and success over your dreams.

Your words can make or break your dreams! Negative, depressing, hopeless words will lead to— negative, depressing, hopeless situations. On the other hand, positive, uplifting, encouraging words will lead to joy and peace and positive results.

When you are on the path toward fulfilling your God-given destiny, you must speak words of life and success over yourself.

Walk in your

God-given purpose.

Work your dreams!

reat songs . . . great books . . . great sermons . . . great businesses . . . great acts of love and kindness . . . great deeds of heroism . . . and great witnesses for the gospel of Jesus Christ are in graveyards—they died without ever having been expressed or established.

Dreams come to pass when we work our dreams and our potential, when we step out and challenge life and take on the possibilities that lie before us. If we are just sitting around thinking about or talking about our dreams and our potential, we will never move into our destiny— we will accomplish nothing and our dreams and our potential will go to the grave with us.

Put sneakers to your faith

and walk out what

you're believing God to do!

Whatever you are believing God to do . . . start working at it!

If you believe God for a business, get a business plan.

If you believe God for a ministry, start studying the Word. Preach in the shower. Preach on the way to work. Preach to your cat and dog. Preach to whoever will listen.

Work your faith!

God has something

ahead for you.

Don't let His dream

die in you!

Be confident that God will complete what He has started in you.

Y ou don't need to know everything. You may never know much of anything. But make sure you know this one thing: The God who started that good work in your life, that same God who gave you your dream, who rescued you from your past, who cleaned up your life, who transformed you and made you a new creation, this same God will complete what He started in you.

Persevere in preparation
for your destiny.

The process of preparation is just that—a process. The journey in this life is just as important as the destination. God does not refine you, train you, transform you, or renew you instantly. He puts you through a process. That process requires patience. It requires a steadfastness and a faithfulness. It requires an ongoing trust and obedience.

You can't prepare yourself in a day. You must prepare
yourself every day . . .

    day after day . . .

        after day after day . . .

           for the rest of your days.

Resources

BOOKS BY PAULA WHITE
- *Deal With It*
- *He Loves Me, He Loves Me Not*
- *Conversations with God Journal*
- *Deal With It Workbook*

DEVOTIONAL GUIDES
- *Daily Treasures*
- *Morning by Morning*

LANDMARK SERMONS
(available in CD or VHS formats)
- *Can You Dig It?*
- *Have You Seen My Resume?*
- *Don't Lose the Evidence*
- *Your Friend Judas*
- *Value of Vision*

All products can be ordered through our eStore or
via our toll-free telephone product line.

www.paulawhite.org

1-800-992-8892